A Secret World of CODES

Dear Reader

Did you know that you and I are using a code to pass on a message right now?

> EVERY DAY, ALL AROUND THE WORLD, PEOPLE USE CODES.

The writing on this page is a code. Once, only a few people knew this code. What code is it? It's the alphabet.

Every day, all around the world, people use codes. Some are secret and some are not so secret. People use codes to pass ideas, money, information and plans to each other.

I hope you enjoy reading about the secret world of codes!

John Parsons

NELSON CENGAGE Learning™
For learning solutions, visit cengage.com.au

Contents

A Secret World of CODES

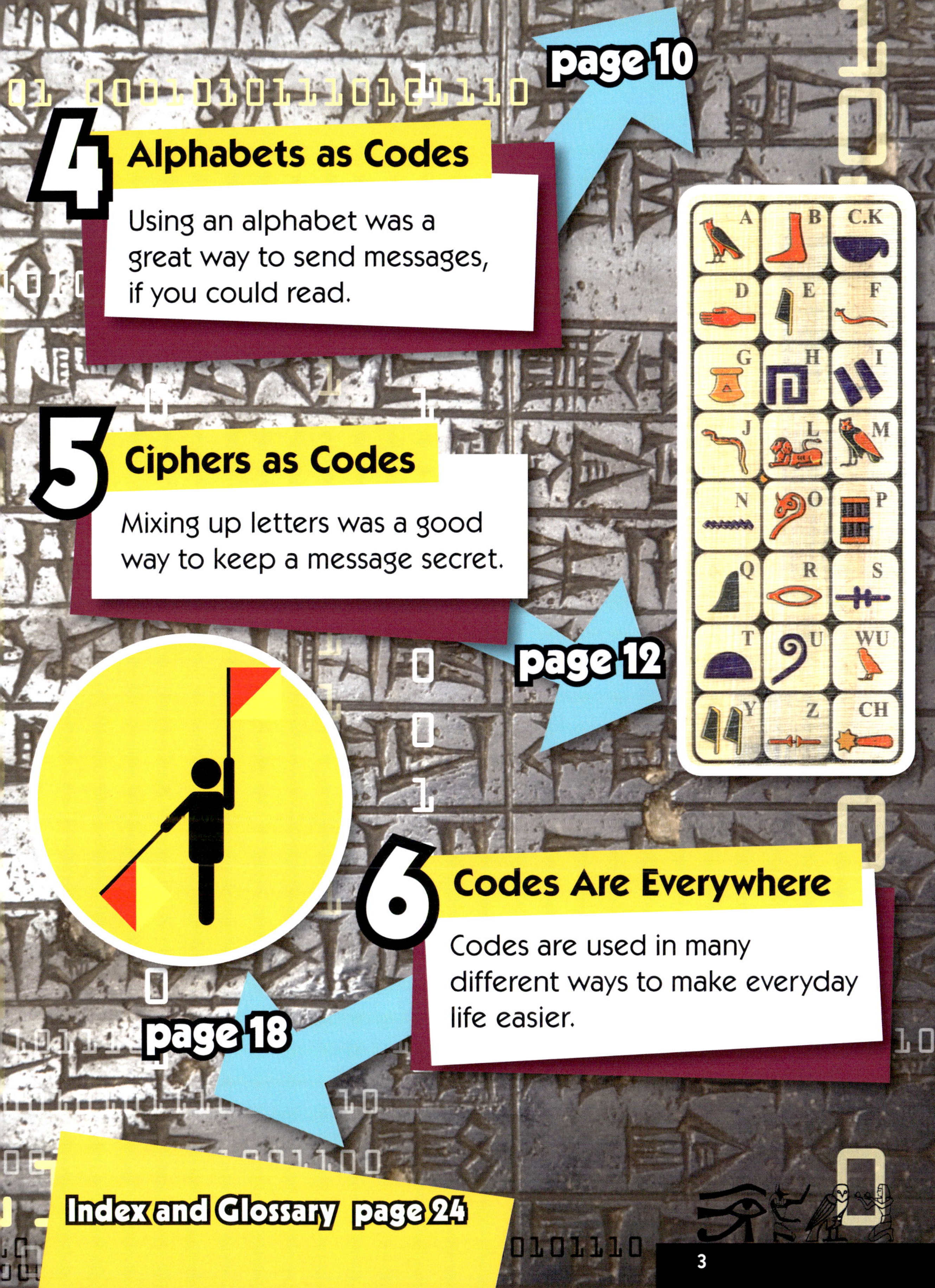

4 Alphabets as Codes

Using an alphabet was a great way to send messages, if you could read.

page 10

5 Ciphers as Codes

Mixing up letters was a good way to keep a message secret.

page 12

6 Codes Are Everywhere

Codes are used in many different ways to make everyday life easier.

page 18

1 The Earliest Codes

Look Out **Behind** You!

People have used codes to pass secret messages to others for thousands of years.

The sounds and words we use in languages are codes. These codes are ancient. We use these codes every day when we speak. Others understand the code because they speak the same language. People who don't speak our language cannot decode what we say.

Tiger Codes

The sounds made by the letters **T-I-G-E-R** are a code. The word is really no more than a sound. But everyone who speaks English understands that this code, or word, means a large, wild cat. It is a useful code, especially if a tiger is creeping up on you!

The same large, wild cat has different codenames in different languages:

- in Russian, the code is: тигр
- in Spanish, the code is: tigre
- in French, the code is: le tigre
- in Mandarin, the code is: 老虎

"Danger! I can see a human!"

Le Tigre!

If a person was yelling, "*le tigre!*" or "*tigre!*" at you and looking frightened, you would probably understand the code, even if you didn't speak French or Spanish. But you might not fully understand if someone from Russia or China was trying to warn you!

A code is like a different alphabet for spelling words. As long as the other person knows that alphabet (or code), they can read and understand the words.

Language

The Very First Language

Between three and four million years ago, the ancestors of modern humans may have used sounds to communicate. Scientists think that "real" language was first used about 40 to 50 thousand years ago.

an image of a human ancestor who lived about three million years ago

Environment

Declining Numbers of Tigers

Less than a hundred years ago, there were around 100 000 tigers in the wild. Now, there are less than 2500.

The hunting of tigers and the destruction of their habitat to provide more land for farming are the main causes of their low numbers.

People are a bigger threat to tigers than tigers are to people.

2 Picture Codes

Stories Use Art Codes

In ancient times, people used art to send messages and tell stories – it was their code. When people saw the pictures they would immediately understand what they meant. Pigments and charcoal were used to draw lines.

Story Codes

Humans started using colours and pigments about 120 000 years ago. By 35 000 years ago, humans could tell stories by painting on cave walls and on rocks.

The first art was a really useful code!

PIGMENTS

Pigments are used to colour something. The first natural pigments would have been made from things in the environment, such as leaves to make the colour green and berries to make the colour red.

an example of early rock art in the USA

Petroglyphs

Paintings or carvings that use symbols carved or painted onto rocks are called "petroglyphs". This word comes from two Latin words – "petro", which means rock, and "glyph", which means symbol or picture.

a petroglyph showing antelopes

This is an example of rock art from Kakadu National Park in the Northern Territory, Australia. It represents an Indigenous legend. The main character is the creation ancestor, Namondjok. *To his right is* Namarrgon *(the lightning man) and the female figure below* Namondjok *is* Barrginj, Namarrgon's *wife. Underneath all three figures is a large family group of men and women.*

Writing is **Faster** Than Drawing

For thousands of years, drawing pictures was a useful code. But drawing pictures could be slow. It might have taken days or weeks to draw a picture or carve it into rocks. People needed a faster code.

Start With Symbols

About 6000 years ago, something changed. People around the world found that they could use lines and curves to represent things, rather than using entire drawings.

For example, as long as everyone knew that the symbol VVVVV VVVVV meant "tiger", there was no need to draw and colour in a whole picture of a tiger. These symbols were the start of writing.

Beware of the VVVVV VVVVV!

This type of writing with symbols is called "cuneiform". It is an example from Iraq and is about 4000 years old.

Common Cuneiform Symbols

= A

= G

= H

= P

= N

= S

= Z

= Q

"Talk" With Codes

People who learnt to write these symbols discovered something very important. They could "talk" using a code that only some people could understand. Codes could now be used to keep things secret from some people while still allowing other people to understand a secret message.

INVENT A CODE

If you had to invent a code using just lines and curves to represent fire, water and corn, what would your symbols look like?

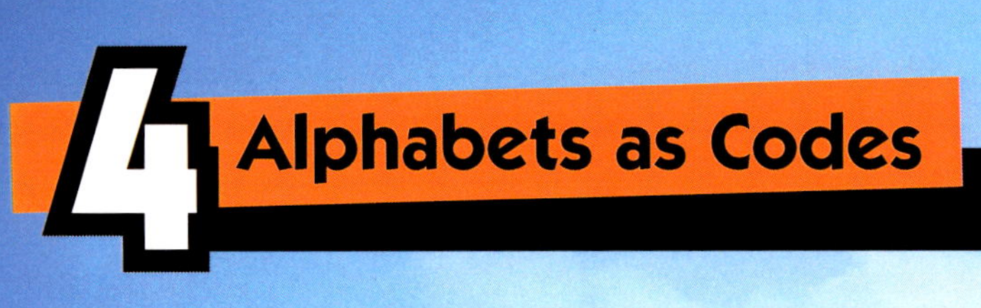

4 Alphabets as Codes

Crack the Secret **Code!**

Alphabets are really just codes for different sounds. But, as people discovered a long time ago, they were a much quicker way of writing than using symbols. Even if you could read symbols, you needed a different symbol for every word.

The First Alphabets

Alphabets were invented in Egypt 4000 years ago. At that time, written codes began to be used by rulers, and by their generals and trusted soldiers. They could send messages to each other without anyone else knowing what they were talking about.

For a long time, ancient rulers could command their armies and rule their lands using writing. But as more and more people learnt how to read and write, it became easier for them to learn about things that others wanted to keep secret.

A new code was needed – a code that *couldn't* be read by just anyone.

00001010100 001010111101

00001010100 00101011110101110 00001 0

Ancient Egyptian Civilisation

Ancient Egyptian civilisation started around 5000 years ago.

As well as written codes, such as hieroglyphics, the ancient Egyptians developed their own umbrellas, soap, board games and glass – and made advances in the fields of medicine, music, mathematics and art.

Being able to communicate well helped the Egyptians succeed in many aspects of their life.

an ancient Egyptian painting of a scene from everyday life

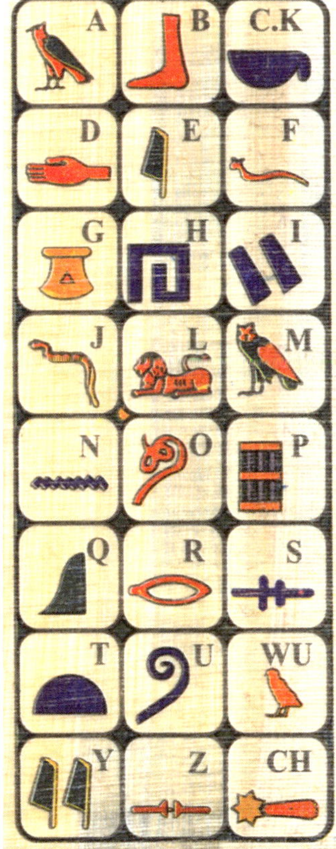

an old Egyptian guide to the alphabet, painted on papyrus

A King's Secret Message

As ruler of his people, a king could send a secret message to his generals telling them to attack his enemies. Even if the enemies found the message, they wouldn't have been able to understand the code.

Use the code guide on the left to decode the message below.

Answer: ATTACK MY ENEMIES

10 00001 0 101 0001010111010110

5 Ciphers as Codes

Disguise **Your** Messages!

Julius Caesar was the leader of the Romans over 2000 years ago. He had a very clever way of disguising his messages. His code used a "cipher". A cipher is a way of mixing up letters so that you scramble the message.

The cipher was kept secret and only Caesar's generals knew how to use it. It was also very, very simple. He just skipped three letters ahead for every letter in his writing!

Instead of writing "A", he wrote "D". Instead of writing "B", he wrote "E". Instead of writing "C", he wrote "F".

Even if people could read, most of them would have had no idea what the message meant!

a statue of Julius Caesar (100–44 BC)

DECIPHER THIS MESSAGE

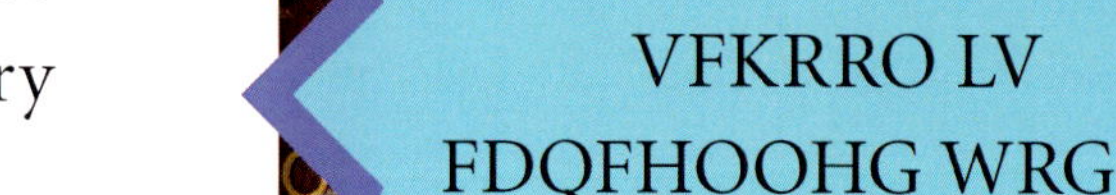

Answer: SCHOOL IS CANCELLED TODAY!

Decipher Tip

The easiest way to decipher the message is to write the alphabet out on the top edges of two pieces of paper, and to shift one piece along by three spaces.

a cipher machine from the 1700s

a Civil War cipher machine from the 1800s

Technology

Cipher Machines

The pictures above show two cipher machines that were used by soldiers in the USA in the 1700s and 1800s. They are now kept in a museum in the National Security Agency in Washington DC, USA. Ciphers are still used today, but they are computerised.

Language and Communication

Deciphering

Deciphering is when we try to work out the meaning of something that may not be clear. Reading a text message is a good example. If someone writes "CUL8R", we decipher its meaning as "see you later".

"What does that mean?"

C	I	P	H	E	R	S
F	L	S	K	H	U	V

Unlock the Codes

Every time a ruler or general wanted to keep messages secret, someone else wanted to find out what those messages meant!

One of those people was a famous Arabian mathematician called al-Kindi. In the 800s, he worked out how to unlock, or break, codes using patterns in language. He knew that certain words were more common than others. This helped him to break codes.

Patterns Help Crack Codes

One example of a common pattern in the English language is the word "the". As it is a very common word, then the most common word in a coded message might also be "the".

There are other things about English that can help you crack a code:

- common letters (E, T, N, O, R, I and A)
- pairs of letters (U almost always follows Q – "quiet")
- word endings (no words end in Q or J in English).

By using information about a language, it is usually possible to crack a simple letter-changing code. Be patient because it can take a long time.

New Codes and Ciphers

Other codes and ciphers were invented almost as quickly as people figured out how to break them! You and a friend can use one of them, with the help of this book. Find out how on page 16.

Morse Code

A	· —
B	— · · ·
C	— · — ·
D	— · ·
E	·
F	· · — ·
G	— — ·
H	· · · ·
I	· ·
J	· — — —
K	— · —
L	· — · ·
M	— —
N	— ·
O	— — —
P	· — — ·
Q	— — · —
R	· — ·
S	· · ·
T	—
U	· · —
V	· · · —
W	· — —
X	— · · —
Y	— · — —
Z	— — · ·

MORSE CODE

Morse code uses dots and dashes to spell words.

the semaphore symbol for "H"

SEMAPHORE

Semaphore uses flags held in different ways to spell out words.

the semaphore symbol for "V"

History

Wig-Wag Signalling

"Wig-wag signalling" (or "wig-wagging") was used in the American Civil War.

A soldier would wave flags to other soldiers from a platform about three metres high.

Unfortunately, this also made him a good target for the soldiers on the other side!

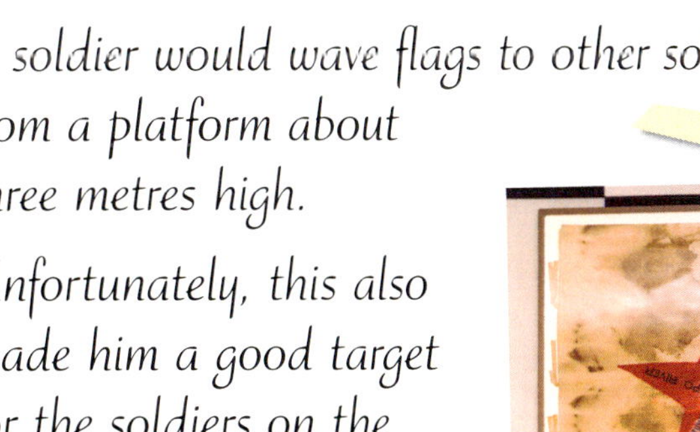

a US army signal flag

a morse code "key"

10 00001 0 101 00010101110101110
00010101110101110

A **Dictionary** Code

One code that is very hard to crack is the "dictionary code".

First, the sender and receiver of the coded message must have the same dictionary. The sender thinks of a message, then finds each word in the dictionary and writes down numbers for the page, column and line. The receiver looks up the page, column and line and finds the word.

History

Dictionary History

The oldest known dictionary, which was discovered in Syria, is a set of tablets over 4300 years old.

The first English dictionary was written by a schoolteacher, Robert Cawdrey, in 1604.

Any books can be used for this code. For example, in this book, the word "tiger" appears on page 8, paragraph 3, line 2, word 1. The code for tiger is therefore 8.3.2.1.

Don't Tell!

As long as you and the receiver don't tell anyone else what book you're using as a code book, this is a very hard code to crack!

It's called a dictionary code because dictionaries have every word you'll ever need. But you can choose your favourite book – and keep it secret!

an American Civil War quilt made by a slave in the 1860s

Social Studies

Quilt Codes

During the American Civil War in the 1860s many African Americans who had been slaves escaped. They used codes to help each other. Quilt codes were a clever way of sending messages. The symbols sewn into the quilts were secret directions to safety. People left the quilts outside as if they were drying in the sun, but really they were secret signs, pointing towards freedom for people trying to escape slavery.

10 00001 0 101 0001010111010110 0001010111010110

6 Codes are Everywhere

Shared Codes **Help Us** Every Day

Today, codes are very common and are used in many ways to help people do things. We need to remember a password or a personal identification number (PIN) to do things like banking or emailing. These passwords or PINs are like electronic codes that tell banks and other organisations who we really are (and whether they should give us our money, for example).

Log On!

When we log on to the Internet, we often use a username, which is a type of code word. Our password with our username is a strong code that is hard to break. Every letter on our computer keyboard also has a code – when we type, the letters are converted into tiny electrical signals that appear on our screen.

USERNAME

A username is a word that can be used to identify us when we are on the computer or Internet. Each username also has a password, which can be a mix of letters and numbers.

What's your password?

PINs

A PIN (Personal Identification Number) is a secret code that can be used to prove that you are who you say you are. PINs can be used at banks, shops and on websites so that someone else cannot pretend to be you. Never tell anyone your PIN.

Mathematics

You'll Never Guess

There are 10 000 different possible number combinations (10 x 10 x 10 x 10) in a four-digit PIN. A six-digit PIN has 1 000 000 different possible combinations (10 x 10 x 10 x 10 x 10 x 10)! That makes it almost impossible for someone to guess your PIN.

Keep bank card PINs secret!

The Internet

Every time someone buys something on the Internet, they can check that their name, address and credit card number will be coded so that no one else can steal it. This sort of code is called encryption.

Emails

Some people send emails over the Internet that are coded, so that only those people who should be reading them can understand them.

Supercomputers

Governments and their armed forces use codes. Instead of strips of alphabets or dictionaries, they use supercomputers to create codes that are almost impossible to break. Supercomputers are very fast and powerful computers that can code and decode messages in millions of different ways.

Kids Having Fun

And, just as they have done for hundreds of years, children around the world use codes, too. You can have some fun with codes on pages 22 and 23!

Language

Encryption

"Encryption" is a word that comes from the ancient Greek word for "hidden" or "secret".

When a credit card number is encrypted, it is mixed up in a way that only the bank can understand, so no one else can steal the real number.

"Will they figure this out?"

an early code computer

a code machine from World War II

"Look, there's another message!"

TOP SECRET FOR KIDS' EYES ONLY

Decipher the Coded Messages

Code 1: ALPHABET NUMBER CODE

Decode the ALPHABET NUMBER CODE coded message!

4-5-1-18 1-7-5-14-20, 4-15 25-15-21 23-1-14-20 20-15 19-5-5 1 13-15-22-9-5 1-6-20-5-18 19-3-8-15-15-12?

TIP

Start by writing out the alphabet and numbering each letter, e.g., A=1, B=2, C=3.

TIP

This works the same way as the ALPHABET NUMBER CODE, but the decoded words may appear backwards.

Code 2: BACKWARDS ALPHABET NUMBER CODE

Decode the BACKWARDS ALPHABET NUMBER CODE coded message!

5-22-1-8 21-15-25 5-14-15-4 18-21-15-25 11-18-15-23-5-13-15-8?

Code 3: SCRATCH NUMBER CODE

Decode the SCRATCH NUMBER CODE coded message!

////-/////////-/////////////////////////-///////////////-
/////////////////////   /////-/-////////////////////

////////////-/////////////////////-//////////////-///-
////////?

TIP

This code works the same way as the ALPHABET NUMBER CODE, but uses scratches (or taps or sounds) instead of numerals.

TIP

Go to page 12 and find out the chapter number. This is the number of letters that have been added to this cipher.

Code 4: PAGE 12 CHAPTER PLUS CODE

Use a cipher to decode the PAGE 12 CHAPTER PLUS CODE coded message!

LTTI BTWP XJHWJY FLJSY!

Code 5: SCRATCH NUMBER CODE

Decode the MORSE CODE message!

—•—• ——— —• ——• •—•

•— — ••— •—•• •— — ••

——— —• •••

TIP

Look carefully for the spaces between the coded letters, or you will get your dots and dashes all mixed up!

Answers

Code 1: DEAR AGENT, DO YOU WANT TO SEE A MOVIE AFTER SCHOOL?

Code 2: HAVE YOU DONE YOUR HOMEWORK?

Code 3: DID YOU EAT LUNCH?

Code 4: GOOD WORK SECRET AGENT!

Code 5: CONGRATULATIONS

Index

Glossary

ancient Greek	The language of a civilisation that existed in Greece and surrounding areas for 1500 years, from about 1000 BCE
Civil War	The war between the northern and southern states of the USA, which lasted from 1861–1865
indigenous	The name given to the group of people who first lived in a country or place
Iraq	A country in the Middle East, where the earliest known civilisation started around 5000 years ago
Latin	The language of the ancient Romans
papyrus	A reed that grows alongside rivers, used to make an early form of paper
slavery	The practice of "owning" another human being, usually to make them work for little or no pay
Syria	A country in the Middle East, where evidence of civilisation has been found from around 3000 years ago